LIFE SKILLS

CONFIDENT COOKING

Rebecca Vickers

Heinemann Library
Chicago, Illinois

www.heinemannraintree.com
Visit our website to find out
more information about
Heinemann-Raintree books.

To order:
☎ Phone 888-454-2279
🖳 Visit www.heinemannraintree.com
to browse our catalog and order online.

Edited by Harriet Milles and Adam Miller
Designed by Philippa Jenkins and Artistix
Picture research by Elizabeth Alexander
Production by Victoria Fitzgerald

Printed and bound in China by South China
    Printing Company Ltd.

13 12 11 10 09
10 9 8 7 6 5 4 3 2 1

**Library of Congress Cataloging-in-Publication
Data**
Vickers, Rebecca.
  Confident cooking / Rebecca Vickers.
    p. cm. -- (Life skills)
  Includes bibliographical references and index.
  ISBN 978-1-4329-2721-9 (hc)
  1. Cookery. 2. Teenagers--Life skills guides.
  I. Title.
  TX652.V52 2009
  641.5--dc22
                        2008047816

Acknowledgments
The author and publishers are grateful to the
following for permission to reproduce copyright
material: © Alamy Images/Eye Ubiquitous/David
Forman/Hutchison Archive p. 25; © Bridgeman
Art Library/British Museum, London, UK/
Topham Picturepoint p. 8; © Capstone Global
Library pp. 9, 46 bottom; © Capstone Global
Library/MM Studios pp. 16, 17 top; © Corbis/
Fancy/Veer p. 18; © Getty Images pp. 28 (Stone/
Judith Haeusler), 5 (Taxi/Julie Fisher), 39 (Todd
Williamson/WireImage), 35 (Walter Hodges/
Stone); © iStockphoto pp. 7 (Chiya Li), 46 top
(Paul Senyszyn), 23 (Serdar Yagci); © Masterfile/
Susan Findlay p. 31; © Photolibrary pp. 12
(Brian Leatart/Foodpix), 27 (Noel Hendrickson/
Digital Vision); © Rex Features/Sipa Press
p. 37; © Science Photo Library/J. L Carson/
Medical Stock Photo p. 20; © Shutterstock pp.
17 (Cathleen Clapper), 48 (Jaimie Duplass), 42
(jocicalek), 47 (Kasia), 33 (Ljupco Smokovski),
11 (Robyn Mackenzie), 34 (Viktor1); © The
International Culinary Schools at The Art
Institutes p. 41.

Cover photograph of a boy throwing pizza
dough reproduced with permission of © Alamy/
Blend Images.

We would like to thank Nicole Clark for her
invaluable help in the preparation of this book.

Every effort has been made to contact copyright
holders of any material reproduced in this book.
Any omissions will be rectified in subsequent
printings if notice is given to the publisher.

Contents

Some words are printed in bold, **like this**. You can find out
what they mean by looking in the glossary.

Why Care About Cooking?

At its most basic level, the human body is a machine that needs fuel in order to function. The liquids we drink and the foods we eat are fuel for the human machine and give it the energy it needs to work. But food is much more than that.

FAMILY, FRIENDS, FELLOWSHIP

People have always gathered together as families, tribes, or communities to eat meals, sometimes with social or religious importance. Cooking and eating as a group was once a way of bonding and showing you trusted one another. After all, you couldn't fight while you were eating. In most cultures, important celebrations from harvests to weddings still include specially cooked foods and the sharing of a meal.

So, why cook?

Food and eating is an important part of any person's daily life. Meals are the way we divide our day and how we come together. But learning to cook is also a basic survival skill. It means you do not have to be dependent on others to provide you with the necessary fuel your body needs. You can cook your food just the way you like it. It also means that you know what you are eating, the food's freshness, and where it comes from.

Learning to cook can also be better for the health of your body and your finances. Having the skills to make a tasty and nourishing snack when you get back from school helps you to avoid the high-salt, fatty, sugary, and expensive treats or fast foods you might be tempted to spend your money on.

It's not rocket science

Since the first of our prehistoric ancestors decided that meat cooked in a fire tasted better than raw meat, human beings have been cooks. Cooking can be as simple as making scrambled eggs or as time-consuming and complex as creating some cakes and sauces. But everyone has to start somewhere to learn this essential life skill. Now it's your chance.

"Cooking is one of the oldest arts and one which has rendered us the most important service in civic life."

Jean-Anthelme Brillat-Savarin (1755–1826), French lawyer, politician, and **epicure**

In recent years in the United States, roughly 32 percent of children were overweight but not **obese**, 16 percent were obese, and 11 percent were extremely obese, according to one study. In Japan, 10 percent of 9- to 11-year-olds are considered to be obese, while in China, the figure is 8 percent. We all enjoy **junk food**, but in later life this could lead to a greater risk of diabetes, heart disease, and cancer. Eating fatty, salty, and sugary foods regularly, in addition to those that are highly **processed** and loaded with food additives, makes the situation much worse.

*There is nothing nicer than cooking food for friends or family to enjoy. It can be a real tribute to your **culinary** skills.*

COOKING CHEMISTRY

Most cooking involves a series of chemical reactions. These occur when different **ingredients** are brought together and subjected to processes (such as stirring or beating) or temperature change. Once these reactions have taken place, they usually cannot be reversed. Your kitchen and its food preparation equipment is like a chemistry lab for cooking.

BOILING AN EGG

For example, when you boil an egg, several chemical reactions take place. As the temperature rises toward the boiling point, changes occur in the raw egg inside its shell. The liquid **protein** in the egg reacts to the temperature change, particularly after it reaches 104°F (40°C), and the egg starts to become solid. The longer the egg is cooked, the more solid the white and yolk become. This is because the rising temperature has caused the protein to break its internal chemical bonds and join into larger **molecules**.

If an egg is boiled long enough, to the point where it becomes "hard-boiled," then it is possible the iron in the egg yolk will react with the sulfur in the amino acids in the egg white and lead to the production of hydrogen sulfide. This can create a smell when you peel and cut open the hard-boiled egg and cause a greenish surface to form on the yolk.

Perfected experiments

So, even a fairly simple cooking task, such as boiling an egg, can be broken down into quite complex chemical reactions. However, in cooking, the chemical experiments that you perform will usually be done using **recipes** in which someone has already tried out and perfected his or her theory of how the cooking reactions will work out. Most really good recipes are the result of someone experimenting and discovering that certain combinations of foods, cooked or reacting together in certain ways, taste great!

*The **raising agent** in these muffins is baking powder (a mixture of sodium bicarbonate and cream of tartar). Carbon dioxide gas is given off during the cooking of the muffin mixture, causing it to rise. Another well-known raising agent is the yeast used in the baking of bread. It also gives off carbon dioxide as it heats up.*

DID YOU KNOW?

Taste is a chemical reaction in your mouth. When you cook, the flavors you combine will create different tastes in the food. If the food is liquid, you will taste it quite quickly as it enters your mouth. If it is more solid, the taste is released as you chew and the food mixes with saliva. The four main tastes the taste buds on your tongue recognize are:

- Sweetness—a chemical reaction to sugars
- Sourness—a chemical reaction to acids
- Bitterness—a chemical reaction to **alkaloids**
- Saltiness—a chemical reaction to sodium chloride and other chlorides.

WHAT DOES IT ALL MEAN?

A recipe contains the "how to" instructions for creating a specific dish. A good recipe should give you all the information you need to recreate a dish. Learning how to follow recipes gives all cooks the chance to make the food they want.

RECIPES THROUGH TIME

Individual cooks have shared recipes with each other for hundreds of years. Families have passed recipes down the generations as part of their oral and written traditions. Ancient manuscripts from the time of the Roman Empire include several books of recipes. From medieval times onward, books of recipes became very popular as rich families competed with each other to produce the most complicated and expensive dishes. In the 19th century, Fannie Farmer in the United States and Isabella Beeton in England produced the first cookbooks for middle-class women to use. During the last 100 years, thousands of cookbooks, covering all of the world's **cuisines**, have been published.

⬇ *This ancient Egyptian figure group from 1900 BCE shows two of the steps in the preparation and baking of bread.*

ROMAN DATES WITH HONEY
This simple recipe would have been served as a dessert after an evening meal in a wealthy household during the time of the Roman Empire. In Latin, dessert was known as the *Secundae mensae*.

Ingredients:
- *12–15 fresh dates (3 for each person)*
- *12–15 walnut halves*
- *3–4 tablespoons of clear honey*
- *Salt and pepper*

Method:
1. Get a sharp knife, a cutting board, and a frying pan.
2. Using the knife carefully (see page 16), peel the skin off the dates, slice each one open on one side, and remove and throw away the date pits.
3. Insert a walnut half into each date where the pit used to be and shake a little salt over the stuffed dates.
5. Put the honey into a frying pan and heat until it has melted.
6. Carefully, on a spoon, lift the dates one-by-one into the hot honey and fry them gently for three to five minutes.
7. Turn off the heat and then, using a spoon, lift the dates one-by-one onto a serving plate. Spoon the honey from the pan over the dates and grind on a little pepper.

DID YOU KNOW?

Good cooks were so highly thought of in wealthy 17th- and 18th-century households that attempts would be made to steal their recipes or get them to change jobs. It was like **industrial espionage** today.

MAKING SENSE OF A RECIPE

Recipes are available from many different sources, including cookbooks, television programs, magazines, newspapers, and the Internet. Most recipes follow a similar format, first giving the ingredients needed for the dish followed by the method to be used to prepare it.

Some recipes will mention specific equipment required to make the dish—for example, a particular size of cake pan or a blender.

Measurements

The list of ingredients in a recipe states the amounts you should use. These measurements have been tested to be correct for the best results. (See the chart on page 43.) It is always sensible to use the amounts listed when you first cook a recipe. The next time you can make small changes if you think the dish would taste better with, for example, a little less sugar. If it works out okay with your alteration, then you can make a note of what you did and cook the dish that way in the future.

If a recipe says that it feeds four people, and you actually want to feed six people, it is generally safe to add half the amount again of each ingredient to your measurements. However, you may need to adjust the cooking time if, for example, the changes in quantity mean that you will need to use a different size or depth of cooking container.

Getting it Wrong

Never use a recipe for the first time if you are cooking for a special occasion, or if it is important that everything goes well. Even experienced cooks can have problems with unfamiliar ingredients or methods. Stick with the things you know you can do well, or practice making the new recipe beforehand.

TIP

Always remember to read through your recipe before you start to cook. You need to be sure you understand all the methods used and have all the ingredients and equipment you need. Also, never start to cook using a recipe that takes two hours when you only have 45 minutes to prepare a meal. People will get hungry!

Once you understand how recipes are laid out, they are easy to follow correctly.

Some recipes state the preparation and cooking time to help you plan ahead.

CHILI: A MEAL IN ONE POT
Serves: 4
Preparation and cook time: 1 hour

Ingredients:
- 2 tablespoons oil
- 1 large onion, chopped
- 1–3 teaspoons of chili powder
- 1 garlic clove, crushed and chopped finely
- 1 pound lean ground beef or ground steak
- 4 tablespoons of tomato paste
- 14-ounce can of chopped tomatoes
- 14-ounce can of kidney beans, drained
- ¼ cup grated cheddar cheese
- 1 small carton of sour cream

This lists the ingredients.

Method:
1. In a large frying pan, fry the onions in the oil over moderate heat until they are soft and transparent. Add the garlic and the chili powder and cook while stirring for one to two minutes.
2. Add the ground beef to the onion mixture and cook until the meat is browned, while stirring constantly.
3. Add the tomato paste, the can of tomatoes (including all the juice), and the kidney beans. If the mixture seems too dry, add water. Simmer for 20 to 30 minutes, adding more water if necessary. Stir occasionally. Serve in bowls and pass around grated cheese and sour cream to top.

Make it veggie! There are two ways to make this dish vegetarian. You can make it exactly as above, but replace the ground beef with a meat-substitute product, or you can skip step 2 and add additional vegetables to step 3, such as a can of drained corn and some peeled and chopped carrots.

Most meat or poultry recipes can be adapted to suit vegetarians.

The "Method" is the order of preparation you should follow.

TIMES AND TEMPERATURES

One of the most important parts of any recipe is the time and temperature given for cooking the dish. Whoever first figured out the recipe experimented with the time and temperature until he or she got it just right. So, what you see on the recipe is the best way to cook the dish. You cannot increase the temperature and cut the cooking time and expect the dish to taste or look just as good.

If you are cooking meat, fish, or other seafood, you must follow the correct cooking time and temperature or it can be dangerous, or even deadly. Uncooked or undercooked meat and fish can contain dangerous **bacteria** (see page 18).

When describing cooking on the stovetop or cooktop, the instructions in recipes usually use the terms "low heat," "medium heat," and "high heat." These are not specific temperatures, but you can figure out what you should do by looking at the knob that turns on each gas burner or electric ring. These commonly have dots around the knob indicating the positions from the coolest temperature to the hottest. You can then turn the knob to choose a position at the lowest for low heat, the middle for medium heat, and the hottest for high heat. Oven temperatures are more specific and easier to get right, as shown on the table on page 13.

Getting it Right

Preheating an oven means turning it on so it can reach the temperature required by the recipe before you put the dish in. Always remember to leave plenty of time for it to get to the correct temperature. On many ovens, a light will either go on or go off to indicate that the temperature you have selected has been reached.

A meat thermometer is a useful way to check that your meat is fully cooked and safe to eat.

Cooking instructions	Fahrenheit	Metric (Celsius, Centigrade)
Very hot	475	245
Very hot	450	230
Hot	425	220
Quick/fairly hot	400	205
Moderately hot	375	190
Moderate/medium	350	175
Warm	325	165
Slow/low	300	150
Very slow/very low	275	135
Very slow/very low	250	120
Very slow/very cool	225	110

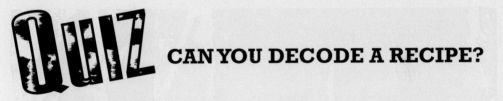

QUIZ CAN YOU DECODE A RECIPE?

1) **The term "ingredients" means:**
   a) the equipment needed for a recipe
   b) the different foods used to make a dish
   c) the method used to cook something.

2) **In degrees Fahrenheit, what would the term "moderately hot" mean?**
   a) 225°F
   b) 320°F
   c) 375°F

3) **When you preheat an oven, you:**
   a) turn it on in time to reach the temperature needed to cook the dish
   b) use the oven to heat up an ingredient before adding it
   c) put a hot dish into a cold oven.

The Cook's Toolbox

The equipment in a kitchen is the toolbox you need for cooking. These supplies can be as simple as a wooden spoon, as high-tech as a microwave, or as exotic as a Moroccan **tagine pot**. Most kitchens will have the majority of the basic things you need.

The Right Tools For The Job

Pans come in all sizes and shapes, made of many different materials. Some have nonstick coatings and others have copper bottoms or even a double-layer construction, which helps the pan to heat more evenly.

It is possible that the recipe you are following will tell you what size or type of pan is best to use (for example, a large frying pan or a **wok**), but not always. When no specific instruction is given, then you have to read through the recipe and figure out what would be best, based on the type of cooking and the amount of ingredients the pan will have to hold.

It is always best to use a pan that is slightly bigger than you need, so the contents are not too near the rim.

• CHECKLIST •

Pots and pans
The following pots and pans are the most commonly needed:

- Saucepan with pouring spout
- Three different sizes of saucepans with lids
- Two different sizes of frying pans
- Large stockpot (for boiling pasta or large quantities)
- Wok
- Round and square cake pans in various sizes
- Toughened glass or ceramic baking dishes
- Roasting pan (with rack)
- Various sizes of baking sheets
- Muffin tin
- Loaf pan
- Pie dish.

• CHECKLIST •

Basic kitchen utensils

This list gives the most commonly used cooking and food preparation **utensils**:

- Knives (see page 16)
- Various wooden, metal, and plastic long-handled spoons
- Slotted spoon
- Ladle
- Potato masher
- Various whisks
- Long-handled fork
- Can opener and bottle opener
- Colander
- Wire mesh sieves/strainers
- Vegetable peeler
- Vegetable steamer basket
- Grater
- Spatulas
- Juicer/squeezer
- Kitchen tongs
- Kitchen scissors
- Rolling pin
- Mixing bowls
- Meat thermometer
- Chopping boards
- Kitchen scale
- Measuring jug
- Measuring cups and spoons
- Kitchen timer
- Cooling racks
- Oven mitt or pot holder.

• CHECKLIST •

Going electric

Some small electrical appliances are efficient and time saving. The following are helpful if you have them available to use:

- Microwave
- Electric mixer
- Blender
- Toaster
- Electric kettle
- Food processor.

Getting it Right

Always be careful when using electric equipment in the kitchen. For example, blenders and mixers have metal blades spinning at high speed, as well as live electricity. Turn off and unplug all electric equipment after use. Cleaning small electrical appliances must always be done without getting the electric components wet. They must NEVER be immersed (soaked) in water.

• CHECKLIST •

Choosing and using knives

Knives are the most important, most widely used, and most dangerous of all the equipment in the kitchen. It is very important that you use a knife safely. Remember these six points and you will be a responsible knife user:

1. It is safest to use good-quality knives made of high carbon stainless steel.

2. Try to use sharp knives. Dull knives are not as good at doing the cutting work, and they are much more likely to slip off the food onto you, leading to injury.

3. Always use the right knife for the job. It can be dangerous to use a small knife for a big-knife task, and vice versa.

4. Be responsible in your knife use. Never swing around with a knife in your hand or pass a knife to other people. Put it down and let them pick it up.

5. Store your knives safely. In a drawer, make sure the handles are at the front. In a countertop knife block or if wall-mounted on a magnetic strip, make sure that they are out of the reach of young children and pets.

6. Never mix sharp knives in with other dirty dishes in a sink. In a dishwasher, never put sharp knives blades upward in the cutlery basket. The safest thing is to wash sharp knives separately by hand after use.

A carving knife is for carving and slicing cooked meat.

A chef's/cook's knife is for all general kitchen work.

A long serrated/bread knife is used for a sawing action, like slicing bread and cutting cake.

A paring knife is for cutting things small and for peeling.

A spatula is for spreading soft substances, such as cake frosting.

SIMPLE FRESH SALSA
Here is a recipe that is all chopping and no cooking!

Ingredients:

- *4 medium-sized ripe tomatoes*
- *6 green onions*
- *A handful of leafy cilantro*
- *4–5 chopped green jalapeños from a jar (optional)*
- *2 tablespoons of lime juice*
- *Salt and ground black pepper*

Method:
1. Get a chopping board, paring knife, chef's knife, and bowl for mixing and serving. Rinse and dry all the vegetables.
2. Finely chop the tomatoes and put them in the bowl.
3. Finely chop the green onions (including some of the green stems) and stir them into the tomatoes.
4. Finely chop the cilantro and stir it into the tomato mixture.
5. Cut up and add the jalapeños (optional; can be quite hot).
6. Add the lime juice and a little salt and pepper to the mixture and stir well.
7. Cover and let the flavors blend for about an hour, and serve with tortilla chips.

Cooking Danger Zones

Anything you eat eventually enters into your body systems. Poor-quality food, or food that has been stored or cooked in a way that lessens its **nutritional value**, will not give you much benefit. However, if food has been allowed to become **contaminated**, that food can be dangerous—and, in the most extreme cases, deadly.

DANGERS IN FOOD

When you buy food, especially fresh food, you expect it to be healthy and fit to eat. Unfortunately this is not always the case. It is possible even for fresh food to be contaminated by **pesticide residue** or bacteria, such as **E. coli** or **salmonella**. Most possible pesticide contamination can be removed by thoroughly washing all fresh fruits and vegetables.

Buying **organic** produce can also remove the threat of pesticide residue, but it will be more expensive.

All foods, even organic ones, can be affected by the bacteria, molds, and yeasts that float in the air and land on surfaces. Natural chemical substances in the food itself, known as enzymes, cause most foods to eventually break down or rot, leading to unpleasant changes in taste, odor, color, texture, and nutritional value.

Food has expiration dates

Any food with packaging has a "use-by" date printed somewhere on it. Check the label before you use the food to make sure it is not past the date, and do not use it if it is. Lots of food also has labeling that tells you how to treat it. Some foods need to be stored in the refrigerator once they are opened. Others tell you how long after opening the item can be kept and the contents safely used. For example, you can keep an unopened jar of mayonnaise in a cupboard, but once it is opened you must put it in the refrigerator. After it is opened, it can generally be used for up to two months, but then whatever is still unused must be thrown away.

Only freeze top-quality food that is in good condition. Never put something in the freezer without first packaging it properly and labeling it with the contents and the date that it went in. No one wants to play the "guess the food" game!

Getting it Wrong

It doesn't do any good to keep food in a refrigerator or freezer if the temperatures are not cold enough to store it safely. The temperature in a refrigerator needs to be between 33–40°F (1–5°C). A freezer needs to have temperatures lower than 0°F (-17°C). Most food should not be kept in a freezer longer than three months, but a number of things, such as some fruits, vegetables, and meat, can be stored frozen for longer.

Storing food correctly extends its use, makes it safer, and maintains its nutritional value. Always check the expiration dates when you choose items to buy.

DANGERS IN THE KITCHEN

As the cook you must also ensure that the kitchen environment itself is safe and hygienic. The equipment and surfaces can harbor all kinds of nasty things and become the breeding ground for illness.

First, make sure all of your utensils and pots and pans are properly washed after use in hot, soapy water or in a dishwasher. Second, clean your countertop surfaces and chopping boards regularly with an anti-bacterial cleaner.

Is your dishcloth deadly?

Experiments have found that one of the main sources of contamination in the kitchen is the dishcloth or sponge used to wipe down countertops. Although it appears that a surface is clean when it has been wiped with a damp cloth, the cloth itself can spread contamination from one place to another.

Some cloths are now available that contain anti-bacterial properties, but no cloth will ever be able to make a surface absolutely contamination free. However, you can do your best by cleaning and replacing your surface cloth or sponge often, rinsing it thoroughly after use in hot, soapy water, and trying to prevent contaminated materials from getting onto kitchen surfaces in the first place.

Are YOU contaminated?

As a cook, you must also consider your personal hygiene and the effects it could have on kitchen safety. Obviously you should wash your hands thoroughly with soap just before you start cooking, but remember also not to touch possibly contaminated areas of your body, especially your nose and mouth, while cooking. Wearing a clean apron is a good idea; it not only protects your clothes from getting dirty, but also protects the food you are preparing from contaminants on your clothing. Tying back long hair and rolling up loose sleeves also helps stop cross-contamination.

This scanning electron micrograph (SEM) image shows some unknown bacteria (in pink) on a kitchen dishcloth!

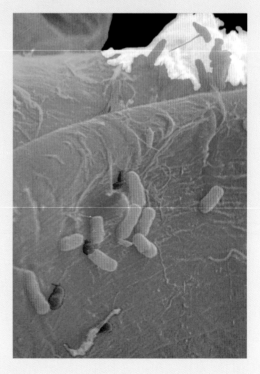

If you use a chopping board to cut up raw chicken and then use the same board to chop up ingredients for a salad, you will cause **cross-contamination**. Even

Getting it Wrong

though the bacteria in the chicken will be killed off if it is cooked properly, the raw salad will have come in contact with that bacteria. It is now contaminated and a danger to anyone who eats it. Cross-contamination can also take place in your refrigerator. If raw meat is not properly packaged, the juices can drip onto other items in the refrigerator. Always check the packaging on raw meat and, to be safe, store it on a low shelf where it has less chance of dripping onto other food.

 **QUIZ**

CAN COOKING BE DANGEROUS?

1) **True or false?**
   A dull knife is always safer to use than a sharp knife.

2) **How long after its "use-by" date can food be safely used?**
   a) three days
   b) no days
   c) one week.

3) **A kitchen counter is clean and hygienic when:**
   a) all the visible material has been thoroughly wiped off
   b) an anti-bacterial spray has been used to clean it
   c) a kitchen counter can never be absolutely clear of all contamination.

Building a Meal

Good ingredients are the building blocks of a tasty meal. Choosing your ingredients and the flavors that combine best with each other is a skill that you will perfect with experience. Each dish in a successful meal should support and complement the others.

FRESH IS FABULOUS . . .

Using really fresh ingredients gives your food an extra helping of taste and nutritional benefits. The colors of the different fruits and vegetables hint at the different minerals and vitamins they contain. Nutritionists now believe we should all eat a "rainbow diet" of different-colored fruits and vegetables to get the correct nutritional balance. The way fruits and vegetables are prepared can also affect their nutritional benefits. To get the most health benefits, remember these hints:

- When appropriate, give your fruits and vegetables a good scrub rather than peeling them.

- Avoid overcooking. Prolonged boiling can break down nutritional elements and also destroy taste.

- Whenever possible, steam or microwave fruits and vegetables.

- Time your cooking so you can serve your food promptly after it is cooked. Important nutrients are lost if food has to sit around waiting to be eaten.

. . . but canned is convenient

In cooking, like other aspects of life, there is a perfect way to do something if we could choose. However, in real life, perfection is often not the most practical choice. Sometimes the preparation of a meal has to be squeezed in between homework and soccer practice. But just because a food is convenient does not mean it has to lack taste or nutrition. For example, canned tomatoes and frozen vegetables are convenient, tasty, and good for you. Similarly, a can of tuna packed in fresh water is convenient and full of protein and healthy fish oils.

TIP

Look for canned and frozen foods that are the least processed and contain the lowest levels of salt and other preservatives. The more added ingredients, the more likely the food is highly processed.

Cooking meals using a wide variety of different colored fruits and vegetables will ensure you get a "rainbow diet" of different nutrients.

OPEN-FACE TUNA MELT
This quick and convenient snack for one is still packed with taste and nutrients.

Ingredients:
- Small can of water-packed tuna chunks
- Slice of whole-grain bread
- 1 tablespoon of light mayonnaise
- Finely chopped pickle (optional)
- 1/8 cup of grated cheese of your choice

Method:
1. Preheat a grill.
2. Drain the tuna and break the chunks up in a small mixing bowl.
3. Mix in the mayonnaise and chopped pickle (optional).
4. Toast the bread on one side under a grill or broiler.
5. Carefully take the bread from under the grill or broiler, turn it over, and spread with the tuna mixture.
6. Top it with the grated cheese.
7. Return to the grill or broiler and cook until the cheese is melted and bubbling. Now it is ready to serve.

BALANCING A MEAL

You will already know about the **MyPyramid food pyramid** and the **five food groups** that make up a balanced diet. These same factors also go into creating a healthy, balanced meal. When you are planning a menu for friends, family, or just for yourself, you need to think of the different food groups and try to make sure you get the balance right.

For example, a meal made up of four different types of steamed vegetables would be tasty, colorful, and rich in certain vitamins, but it would contain no protein or **carbohydrates**. Add some beans or cooked chicken and serve your new mixture over a portion of rice and you have a balanced main course. Follow it up with a fresh fruit salad served with natural yogurt and you have a perfectly balanced meal.

A healthy balance means eating the most of those foods containing whole grains, fruits, vegetables, and fish; eating in moderation cheese, milk, eggs, nuts, poultry, and meat; and eating only small amounts of sugars, oils, butter, and salt.

DID YOU KNOW?

A vegetarian is someone who does not eat the flesh of animals. A vegan does not eat animal flesh, nor anything that comes from animals— such as eggs, milk, cheese, all other dairy products, and honey. Always ask any guests you are cooking for if they have any special dietary requirements.

Hidden fats, sugar, and salt

When you use fresh ingredients in your cooking, you pretty much know what you are getting. You can see the excess fat on a piece of meat and can cut it off. You can control how much salt you shake over your food or how much sugar you add to a dish.

But some processed food products contain high levels of sugars, fats, and salt without it being obvious. For example, some brands of canned soup are high in salt. Many of the sauces and condiments you can buy, including some brands of ketchup, are high in sugar and salt. So-called "juice drinks" often contain only small amounts of fresh fruit juice and large amounts of sugar. When creating balanced meals, always check labels on food products to make sure that hidden ingredients don't sneak in!

Can you be a "green" cook?
Yes, you can. All you need to remember
is what products have to travel the farthest
to get to you. This tells you how many "food miles"
the product has added to your **carbon footprint**. Try to use fewer
of the ingredients that travel the most food miles. You can also
decrease your carbon footprint by using local food when it is in
season. If you have to buy food that has traveled long distances,
try to go for "fair trade" brands that do not exploit the agricultural
workers in developing countries.

Some foods, such as these bananas, have to travel thousands of miles from the tropical countries where they grow to reach stores in other parts of the world. This does not necessarily mean that we should not buy them, but we should try to choose "Fair Trade" brands when we do.

MAKING A MEAL PLAN

When you have figured out the balanced meal you want to cook, have gathered all your ingredients, and made sure you have all the kitchen equipment you need, you will still need a plan of action. How easy or how difficult this will be depends on the number of different dishes and courses you are making. When planning a meal, you need to analyze the time each step in the preparation will take so that all the components of the dish will be ready at the same time. For example, it is not a good idea to boil your pasta before you make the sauce, or make your icing before you bake the cake.

Critical path analysis

Critical path analysis is a management technique developed to help people to schedule and organize complex tasks. The three main steps used in

critical path analysis can also help you with your meal plan checklist:

- Make a work breakdown schedule of all the activities you need to undertake to complete your task.

- Figure out the length of time that each activity takes.

- Figure out the "dependencies" between any of the activities. "Dependencies" mean when the ability to do one task is dependent on having already done another. For example, putting potatoes on to cook is dependent upon having first washed and/or peeled them.

The longest "path" in any complex task is the one around which all the other tasks get done. This is the critical path. If you were making a roast chicken dinner, the time it takes to prepare and cook the chicken would be the critical path around which the preparation and cooking of the vegetables, potatoes, and gravy that go with it would be organized.

↑ *A meal plan or checklist can help you get all your cooking finished at the same time when you are preparing a meal.*

QUIZ CAN YOU PLAN A MEAL?

1) True or false?
When you make a healthy meal, never use canned food.

2) The best way to achieve a healthy, balanced meal is to:
a) include elements from the five food groups
b) cook only fruits and vegetables
c) never have dessert.

3) Critical path analysis is a technique for:
a) yard maintenance
b) organizing complex tasks
c) criticizing your meal plan.

Outdoor Cooking

Somehow, food cooked and eaten outdoors always tastes better. Whether it is in your own backyard, at a campsite next to your tent, or in a remote wilderness, outdoor cooking leaves you wanting more.

BACKYARD BARBECUES

Barbecues have become a common fixture in many people's lives. Whether you cook on charcoal or on a gas grill, that barbecue-grilled flavor is hard to get any other way. Although meats, such as burgers, sausages, and chicken, are the most common barbecue food, vegetables, fish, and baked potatoes can all be successfully cooked on an outdoor grill.

Fruit on fire

Recently, grilling fruit has become a popular way to create a barbecue sweet treat. Slices of fresh pineapple, whole bananas, strawberries, and chocolate wrapped in foil and mixed fruit **kebabs** have now joined marshmallows as barbecue desserts.

Everyone can be a chef at a backyard barbecue, and no one seems to mind if the food is a bit burned!

FRUIT KEBABS
This recipe will make four kebabs.

Ingredients:
- *8 large strawberries*
- *Thick, peeled banana pieces*
- *Pitted peach halves*
- *Fresh pineapple chunks*
- *Small tub of natural yogurt*
- *2 tablespoons of clear honey*

Method:
1. Push the fruit pieces onto four metal skewers, alternating fruit types
2. Place on the grill and cook for three to four minutes, turning often. Make sure to use an oven mit or a pot holder.
3. Remove from the grill and serve with a dipping sauce made of the yogurt and honey mixed together.

Getting it Wrong

When you are lighting charcoal in your grill, never use gasoline to speed it up. This is a particularly dangerous thing to do when the charcoal is already lit, as the fire can run up the stream of gasoline and cause the container to explode in flames. If you are using a special charcoal lighter fluid, follow all of the instructions. Every year, people using inappropriate **accelerants** on charcoal end up in the hospital with serious burns. Don't become one of them!

TIP

Never cook meat on a grill when it is too hot, or, in the case of charcoal, still flaming. The outside of the meat will cook quickly and seal the raw meat inside. If the meat is contaminated with bacteria, such as E. coli, it will be dangerous to eat. Food poisoning causes unpleasant vomiting and diarrhea in a healthy person, but can kill the very young, the old, and people with impaired **immune** systems. If meat is grilled at the right temperatures for the correct length of time, any dangerous bacteria will be destroyed.

CAMPFIRE COOKING

If you camp at a campsite, there will often be grills there for your use, or you can take your own portable or disposable grills. If a fire pit is provided, you can take the opportunity to experiment with campfire cooking. If there is no fire pit, and campfires are allowed, you will need to clear away material that could burn and, if possible, make your own fire pit, marking its boundary with large stones. If you have permission to do so, collect your own wood. If not, you will have to bring wood with you. After you have built your fire, you can cook over it in a variety of ways:

- Wrap food items in aluminum foil. Place the foil packets directly on the glowing embers of the burning wood using a long-handled utensil.

- Bring a grill rack that you can put across the fire and place the food on.

- Make a tripod stand out of **green wood** and hang a cooking pot from it.

- Make a hanging rail. Do this by running a long, strong, straight green wood branch parallel to the ground across the top of two strong upright sticks with forked tops. You can hang a cooking pot from the rail.

- Strip the bark from some long, straight green wood branches. Thread food items onto the branches and hold them over the flames to cook the food.

Popular campfire food

Food that cooks well in foil packets includes baked potatoes, corn on the cob, carrots, most white fish (such as cod or haddock), and ground beef mixed with various other ingredients. All normal barbecue food will cook on a grill rack over an open wood fire in the same way as it would cook over charcoal or gas. Cooking-pot favorites include soups, stews, and chili.

TIP

When you cook food in foil packets in the embers of a campfire, sprinkle water over the food first and add a little butter or oil. Season to taste and seal the packet securely by folding and then crimping the edges on top. Make sure the packet is still loose around the food so that the steam from the water can help it cook. None of the flavors or nutrients will be able to escape.

Hot dogs, sausages, chicken pieces, and marshmallows will all cook when skewered onto branches and held over a fire.

→

A campfire is a big responsibility. Never, ever build a fire unless you have permission and have some way of putting it out. You can do this using water, sand, or soil. Also, never build a fire in strong winds or in an area suffering from excessive dryness or drought. Before you leave it, make absolutely sure the fire is completely out with no embers that the wind could blow back to life.

Getting it Wrong

FOOD IS A WINDOW ON THE WORLD

Many people today get more opportunity to travel the world than their grandparents did. But even if you cannot visit some places you would like to, you can still get a taste of what they are like by cooking their national dishes.

CHOOSE YOUR CUISINE

For the last 100 years, the most respected and copied style of cuisine by top restaurant chefs has been French cuisine. Although most award-winning restaurants do not call themselves "French," the food they cook, and often the training of the chefs, has been in classic French cooking.

Beef stew by another name

One of the most popular French dishes outside France is Boeuf (beef) Bourguignon, which comes from the Burgundy region of France. You will be able to find many recipes for this classic French beef stew recipe on the Internet. Another French influence has been the use of cooked sauces. The most famous of these is white sauce, which is the basis for many other sauces containing added ingredients. A recipe for white sauce is on page 46.

Food from the old country

Another way international cuisines have spread around the world to our kitchens has been through immigration. For example, most large cities outside China have a "Chinatown" district, with restaurants and Chinese supermarkets. This is because when Chinese people left their homes to settle in other countries they set up their own restaurants and markets. To begin with, these were for the newly arrived immigrants. Eventually these restaurants attracted local people, and an appreciation of the Chinese cuisine spread. Today, lots of people outside China regularly eat Chinese dishes. Many people have a Chinese stir-fry pan, known as a wok, in their kitchens.

DID YOU KNOW?

On page 7, we listed the four basic tastes that your tongue recognizes. Those who regularly eat Chinese and other Asian cuisines believe there is a fifth taste, known as *umami*. This is the recognition of the taste caused by glutamic acids or glutamates. *Umami* is a Japanese word meaning "deliciousness."

GARLIC BROCCOLI IN HOISIN SAUCE
This is a very simple Chinese vegetable dish.

Ingredients:
- *6 cups of blanched (boiled a few minutes) broccoli, separated into small pieces (florets)*
- *1 tablespoon of vegetable oil (not olive oil, as it will smoke)*
- *3 finely chopped, peeled garlic cloves*
- *3 tablespoons of water*
- *1 small jar of hoisin sauce*

Method:
1. Heat the oil in a wok. Use a large frying pan if you don't have a wok.
2. Add the broccoli and chopped garlic to the wok. Stir-fry at a medium heat for four to five minutes.
3. Add 2 tablespoons of the hoisin sauce and the water.
4. Stir-fry until the broccoli is cooked. Add a bit more water if necessary. Serve hot with rice or egg noodles.

Chopsticks are often offered to you in Chinese restaurants. If you are making Chinese food at home, try to use chopsticks. It isn't as hard as you might think!

→

National cuisines go international

The most popular international cuisines that people like to cook in their own homes are Italian and Mexican. Most people now do not even think of pasta and pizza as being Italian, as they are such an accepted part of many people's diets. Recently, Thai food has also become very popular, and some home cooks are getting brave enough to try to make Japanese dishes. In the United States, the increased popularity of sushi has inspired many people to try to create their own sushi at home.

FAJITAS

Ingredients:
- *Warmed flour or corn tortillas*
- *Strips of grilled chicken or steak—or both!*
- *Package of fajita spices*
- *A mix of chopped-up fresh peppers, onions, and tomatoes*
- *Jalapeño peppers from a jar*
- *Guacamole (see recipe on page 47)*
- *Sour cream*
- *Salsa (see recipe on page 17)*
- *Grated cheese*

(Use amounts suitable to the number of people you are serving.)

Method:
1. Sprinkle the meat with the dry fajita spices and then grill or pan-fry.
2. Stir-fry all the chopped vegetables in a little vegetable oil, using a wok or large frying pan.
3. Mix the cooked meat into the vegetable mixture (keep some vegetable mix separate for any vegetarian guests). Add more spices if you like it hot.
4. Lay out all of the other accompaniments—tortillas, peppers, guacamole, sour cream, salsa, and grated cheese—and let your guests fill and roll their own tortillas with whatever they like.

From Mexican to Tex-Mex

When a cuisine becomes international, it often gets altered as the cooks in the new countries make changes or invent dishes to suit the new country's style. This definitely happened with the "Chinese" dish Chop Suey, which actually developed in San Francisco in California, not in China.

The mixing of different food styles on the border between Mexico and the state of Texas has created a cuisine that many people love, known for the last 35 years as Tex-Mex. Many well-known dishes, such as fajitas, are in fact Tex-Mex, not Mexican cuisine. In fact, fajitas were first served in their current form at a restaurant in Texas in 1969.

Think about how you could make your own special changes to the fajitas recipe on page 34. It is a perfect choice for an informal meal with friends or family.

Every night when you sit down to eat, you can travel the world through your meal.

DID YOU KNOW?

Many of the spices now used widely in the western world did not arrive with immigrants from other lands. They were first brought back from the Middle East to Western Europe by soldiers returning from the Crusades in the 12th century. After that time, the huge demand for spices was one of the spurs to the age of exploration. This eventually led to the mapping of the world. The desire for tastier food really did change history!

CAREERS IN COOKING AND CATERING

Cooking for yourself can be fun and sociable. It can give you independence and help your finances. But it could also become an important part of your future. Cooking could be a career choice.

WHAT JOBS ARE OUT THERE?

Cooking as a career covers everything from working in a fast food restaurant to a position in a five-star restaurant. You can train specifically in mass catering for the hotel, education, or airline industries. You can work for the prison system, the military, or in hospitals. There are cooking jobs for all levels of skills and expertise.

Training for the job

When you are still in school, you might have an opportunity to take some cooking classes as part of home economics. After high school, you might want to consider going to a culinary school. If you are particularly adventurous, you might consider learning a particular cuisine in its native environment—for example, studying French cooking in Paris.

DID YOU KNOW?

Most large professional kitchens have very specific jobs for different cooks. Here are some of them:

- Head chef (Chef de cuisine)—the boss of the kitchen
- Sous chef—second in command
- Station chef—someone in charge of a specific food preparation area in a kitchen
- Prep chef—apprentice or trainee in a specific area. In large professional kitchens a prep chef will go through three to four years of gradual training.
- Saucier—chef who works only with sauces
- Pastry chef—chef who only works on pastries
- Communard—chef in charge of making the meal for all the kitchen's staff at the end of a shift.

Some colleges offer courses studying the catering and food industries, often with business and management options. These areas of study can lead to degrees in various areas related to food, catering, and the hospitality industry.

Working your way up

You can get an entry-level job in a professional kitchen—for example, in a restaurant or hotel—and train on the job like an **apprentice**. These jobs are often advertised as being for a "kitchen assistant" or "trainee chef" and sometimes involve classes at local colleges. Other entry-level jobs are often prep chef positions.

TIP

If you think you may be interested in a career in cooking or catering, try to get a part-time or Saturday job in a related field. See if you can get an internship or even visit different cooking environments. You may be able to figure out what kind of cooking jobs, if any, appeal to you as a future career.

In a busy professional kitchen each person has a specific job to do and has to keep out of everyone else's way. This is not always easy in cramped, hot surroundings, and it can be very stressful.

BEING A CHEF AND A CELEBRITY

Careers in cooking have hit the headlines with the popularity of cooking-related programs on television. Some demonstrate how to cook various dishes, some are **reality television** shows about real restaurants, and some are cooking game shows. Many of these programs have made stars of the people who appear on them.

From footballer to celebrity chef

One of the most popular of the current celebrity chefs is Gordon Ramsay (born 1966). But Ramsay didn't start out wanting to be a chef. As a teenager he wanted to be a soccer player. By the age of 17 he was on the youth team of a professional soccer team in Scotland. However, his dream of a career in soccer was ruined by injury, and at age 19 he left the sport. He says he ended up at catering college "by accident." No matter how it happened, his skills in his "accidental" career have taken him to the top, and made Ramsay one of the most influential chefs on the planet.

Until only a few years ago, Ramsay was just a respected professional chef, but not a household name. Then, in 2004, came his first television series. His programs are now watched all over the world. His success as a media star has increased interest in his professional career. He has now opened restaurants around the world.

Influencing what people eat and more: Emeril, Rachael, and Jamie

In recent years other celebrity chefs have had an influence on what and how people eat. Many famous chefs have hosted successful TV programs, and recipe books of the dishes from their shows have become bestsellers.

Beyond hosting entertaining shows, celebrity chefs can make a difference. In 2002 U.S. chef Emeril Lagasse developed a foundation that works to help underprivileged children. The organization has given children's charities millions of dollars. In 2006 U.S. chef Rachael Ray developed a nonprofit organization aimed at promoting healthy eating habits among young people. Similarly, British chef Jamie Oliver used a television show to advocate the need to improve the quality of school meals in the United Kingdom. His show directly led to improvements in these meals.

DID YOU KNOW?

Whenever a new cook book by a television celebrity chef comes out, grocery stores notice an increase in the sale of the particular ingredient mentioned in the book.

Gordon Ramsay is now better known as a straight-talking TV celebrity chef than for his award-winning restaurants.

➜

Are You a Confident Cook?

You now have some idea of all the things you will need to learn, practice, and perfect in your journey to become a self-sufficient cook. The chemistry of cooking, the specific language, the equipment used, and the techniques you will need to acquire are all parts of this important life skill.

Is There a Kitchen in Your Future?

Of course there is a kitchen in everyone's future—we all need to eat! But it could become something more to you if you decide on cooking as a career. However, you do not need to commit your whole life to cooking to enjoy it. Many people get great satisfaction from cooking as a hobby. Some people like to become experts in one particular aspect of cooking, such as bread-making, cake decorating, jam making, or the cuisine of a particular country. Maybe wilderness or campfire cooking is something you could develop an interest in.

Confidence to experiment

Once you have gained some experience and become familiar with the basic cooking techniques, you can start to change and improvise recipes, and even invent your own. These experiences will help you build confidence in your cooking skills.

Experimenting with tastes, flavors, and methods will sometimes create new masterpieces and at other times, disasters. Don't let yourself get discouraged if the occasional dish gets left uneaten—trial and error is the only way to learn new skills. And who knows, one day you may prove your mastery of confident cooking and produce a recipe that is delicious and completely unique to you.

DID YOU KNOW?

If you are interested in improving your cooking skills, or becoming a specialist in one area of cooking, there are classes you can take. Some are run by private cooking schools and others as continuing or adult education courses. There are also residential vacations or camps you can go on to learn special cooking skills.

> "I feel a recipe is only a theme, which an intelligent cook can play each time with a variation."
>
> Madame Jehane Benoît (1904–1987), Canadian cook and author

In 2008 Jonathan Miller won a national competition for teenage chefs in the United States. The finals were broadcast on the Food Network, and he also was awarded money toward college tuition fees.

COOKING EGGS

Eggs are nourishing and versatile, and can be cooked in many ways.

Poaching eggs

Eggs can be poached in a special egg-poaching pan or in boiling water in a shallow saucepan or frying pan. To do this, crack the egg into a cup or small bowl. Then carefully slide the egg into water that is simmering, but not at full boil. Cook for about three minutes and lift it out gently in a slotted spoon.

Frying eggs

Eggs can be fried in a small amount of cooking oil in a frying pan. In a nonstick pan you will need less oil. Heat the oil over moderate heat. Crack the egg into a cup or bowl and then pour it into the frying pan. It will take two to four minutes to cook, depending on how solid you like the yolk. To cook the yolk, you can either flip the egg over halfway through the cooking time or use a metal spoon to baste the yolk with some of the hot oil during the cooking time.

Scrambling eggs

Crack two to four eggs into a bowl and beat them well with a fork or whisk. Melt a piece of butter in a small frying pan or saucepan until the butter starts to bubble. Turn the heat to low and add the egg mixture to the pan, stirring all the time until the egg has started to firm up. Remove from the heat, keep stirring, and add any extras you want, such as cream, grated cheese, or chopped herbs.

Omelette

Crack two to four eggs into a bowl and whisk until the mixture is light and frothy. Heat a small piece of butter over moderate heat in a frying pan until it is bubbling, but do not let it brown or burn. Add the egg mixture to the pan. Carefully holding the pan by its handle, lift it slightly above the heat, and tip and turn it in a circular movement so the egg mixture is at the pan's edge.

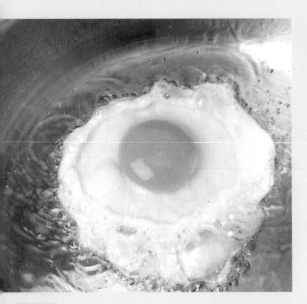

Fried eggs can be "sunny-side up" like this one, or flipped to cook on both sides.

Continue this movement until all of the egg seems set and lightly cooked. The top of the omelette can be finished off under a hot broiler or grill, which will make it rise. When cooked, the omelette can be folded over and carefully lifted onto a plate for serving. Omelettes are often served with a filling folded inside. Suggested fillings are: grated cheese, chopped bacon, sliced and cooked mushrooms, chopped cooked meat, or vegetables. Herbs are best added to the egg mixture before cooking. Some people like a sweet filling such as jam, honey, or sweetened fruit.

TIP

Never eat raw or undercooked eggs. Eggs can carry the salmonella bacteria, which is only destroyed by cooking. Wash your hands thoroughly after handling eggs and egg mixtures.

Cooking measurement conversion chart

Most recipes in U.S. cookbooks today use imperial measurements (pounds and ounces) and teaspoon, tablespoons, and cups. Outside the United States, most cookbooks use the metric system.

This chart converts the systems. Some cookbooks give more than one system of measuring the ingredients, but you should never mix the systems when preparing a recipe. Choose one and stick with it.

Milliliters (ml)	Fluid ounces (fl. oz.)	Cups (c)	Tablespoons (T or tbsp)	Teaspoons (t or tsp)
15 ml	½ oz.	⅛ cup	1 tbsp	3 tsp
30 ml	1 oz.	¼ cup	2 tbsp	6 tsp
50 ml	2 oz.	⅓ cup	4 tbsp	12 tsp
75 ml				16 tsp
	3 oz.	½ cup	6 tbsp	18 tsp
125 ml	4 oz.		8 tbsp	24 tsp
	5 oz.	½ cup	10 tbsp	30 tsp
150 ml		⅔ cup		32 tsp
175 ml	6 oz.	¾ cup	12 tbsp	36 tsp
250 ml	8 oz. (½ pint)	1 cup	16 tbsp	48 tsp
500 ml	16 oz. (1 pint)	2 cups		
1 liter	32 oz. (2 pints or 1 quart)	4 cups		

Note: A "dash" or a "pinch" are generally considered to be less than ⅛ teaspoon.

COOKING POTATOES

Potatoes can be put into two groups: small "new" potatoes, harvested and eaten in the summer months, and larger "old" potatoes that have been left in the ground to grow and are available throughout the year. Old potatoes are best for roasting, baking, making French fries, and mashing. New potatoes are best with salads and summer foods. Potatoes can be cooked in many ways to have with a meal or as a meal in themselves. NEVER use potatoes that are sprouting or have green skins. These contain a powerful toxin (poison) that can make you sick.

Roast potatoes

Peel the potatoes and cut them into even-sized pieces so they will cook at the same rate. Put them in a saucepan, cover with hot water, and bring to a boil for three to five minutes. Drain them well so they are no longer wet. At this point they can either be added to the hot fat around roasting meat, or poultry, or cooked separately on a baking sheet containing a little oil, margarine, or meat dripping that has been preheated in the oven at 400°F (200°C). Be careful when you add the potatoes to the hot oil! Any water on the potatoes will cause the oil to spit up, and you could get burned. It will take about 40 to 60 minutes for potatoes to roast, depending on their size.

Mashed potatoes

Peel the potatoes, cut them into pieces, and boil in water for about 15 minutes until soft. Drain the potatoes and return them to the saucepan. Mash until smooth with a potato masher or a fork. Gradually add milk and some butter or margarine and mix well. Do not add too much milk or the potatoes will be runny rather than fluffy.

New potatoes

These small baby potatoes only need washing, not peeling. Put them in a pan and cover with boiling water. Bring them back to a boil and simmer for 10 to 15 minutes until tender. Drain and serve with butter and some chopped parsley.

Baked potatoes

Use potatoes that are the same medium-to-large size and have skins that are in good condition. Preheat the oven to 400°F (200°C). Scrub the potatoes well and cut off any bad patches. Carefully stab the potatoes several times with a fork. Put directly onto the oven rack and cook for about 45 minutes for medium potatoes or 1 hour for large potatoes. Serve with butter or margarine, or with fillings or toppings, such as sour cream, grated cheese, fried onions, tuna salad, cottage cheese, or chili (see page 11).

VEGETABLES

All fresh vegetables have different methods for their preparation and cooking. You can find directions in cookbooks or by looking on the Internet. Here are several general tips that relate to all types of vegetables.

- Try to buy fresh vegetables and use them as soon as possible. They can lose nutritional value even when still fit to eat.

- Many vegetables that we peel, such as carrots and potatoes, contain a lot of nutritional value in their skins, or near the surface, so just scrub if possible. If you need to peel, try to scrape off just the very outside, rather than peeling off a thick layer.

- Vegetables cooked in water lose vitamins into the water, which is usually drained away. Whenever possible, cook vegetables in a steamer basket or in a microwave.

- Don't overcook vegetables or, once again, you risk losing taste, texture, and nutritional value.

COOKING RICE

Everyone has their favorite way to cook rice, and most cookbooks list two or three methods. A quick and simple way to cook long-grained rice is called the "2-to-1" method. You simply add double the amount of water to the amount of rice used. The measurements can be made using any glass or cup. This is enough rice for two to three people as an accompaniment.

Ingredients:
- *1 large teacup of long-grained rice*
- *2 large teacups of water*
- *A piece of butter*

Method:
1. In a pan with a tight-fitting lid, heat the butter until it bubbles.
2. Add the teacup of rice and stir until the rice grains are coated in the butter and have become transparent.
3. Add the water and bring to a boil over high heat.
4. When the rice is boiling, stir it once and put on the lid.
5. Turn down the heat to as low as possible and cook for 15 minutes.
6. Take off the heat and let it sit with the lid still on for 5 minutes before serving.

COOKING PASTA

All dried pasta needs to be cooked in large amounts of boiling water and then be well drained after cooking. Check on the package for the recommended boiling time. Spaghetti and linguine will take less time to cook than pasta twists or bows. Whole-grain (brown) pasta will take slightly longer to cook. Fresh pasta (available from most supermarkets) takes less time.

BASIC WHITE SAUCE (ROUX SAUCE)

A white sauce, also known as a roux sauce, is the foundation for other sauces, such as mornay, béchamel, and cheese sauces. This recipe shows you how to make 1¼ cups of basic "coating" (thick) white sauce.

Ingredients:
- 1¾ tbsp butter or margarine
- ¼ cup all-purpose flour
- 1¼ cup milk

Method:
1. Heat the butter in a medium saucepan until it has melted.
2. Stir the flour into the butter and cook it for two to three minutes, stirring continually. Do not let the mixture brown.
3. Gradually stir in the milk, preferably using a whisk.
4. Bring the sauce to a boil and then turn down to a low heat and keep whisking until it has thickened. Season to taste.
5. For a thinner sauce, add more milk, and for a very thick sauce, use less milk.

GUACAMOLE

Use this as a dip for corn chips or serve as part of a dish like fajitas (see page 34).
Serves: 6–8 as a dip
Preparation time: 30 minutes

Ingredients:

- *3 ripe avocados, peeled and halved*
- *1 small onion, finely chopped*
- *2 tomatoes, peeled, deseeded, and finely chopped*
- *1–2 red chili peppers, deseeded and finely chopped*
- *1 handful of fresh cilantro, chopped*
- *3 tablespoons of lemon juice*

Method:

1. In a medium bowl, mash the avocado flesh. Add the tomatoes, chilis, and onions and stir well.
2. Add the cilantro and the lemon juice and mix again.
3. Spoon into a serving bowl. If not serving immediately, cover tightly and refrigerate or the mixture will discolor.

NEVER touch your eyes, lips, or nose after chopping chilis! You may suffer a severe reaction. Wash your hands thoroughly after touching or chopping chilis.

TIP

STUFFED PEPPERS
Serves: 4
Prep and cook time: 1 hour
Preheat oven: 400°F (200°C)

Ingredients:
- *4 large bell peppers*
  (make sure they can stand up!)
- *1 large onion*
- *1 tablespoon of cooking oil*
- *⅓ pound lean ground beef*
- *2 tomatoes*
- *2 tablespoons of tomato paste or tomato ketchup*
- *4–5 tablespoons of cooked rice*
- *¾ cup grated cheddar cheese*

Method:
1. Wash the peppers thoroughly. Cut off the tops and clean out the seeds.
2. Place the peppers in a saucepan of water, bring to a boil, and then simmer for five minutes. Carefully lift the peppers out of the saucepan with tongs, making sure all the water inside the peppers has drained out.
3. Place the cooked peppers upright in a baking dish and set aside.
4. Chop up the onion and fry it in a little hot oil.
5. Add the meat to the onions and cook until browned.
6. Cut up and deseed the tomatoes and add to the meat mixture.
7. Add the tomato paste and the cooked rice and warm through. If mixture seems dry add 1 to 2 tablespoons of water.
8. Take off the heat and spoon the mixture into the peppers.
9. Add 2 tablespoons of water to the bottom of the baking dish and carefully place it in the center of the preheated oven.
10. Cook for 20 minutes and then remove, add grated cheese to the top of the peppers, and replace in the oven until the cheese bubbles (three to four minutes).
11. Serve with corn and a salad.

Make it veggie! Replace the beef with ground vegetables or cooked brown lentils.

MACARONI AND CHEESE

Prep time: 15 minutes
Cook time: 30 minutes
**Preheat oven: 400°F
(200°C)**

Ingredients:

- ½ pound dried macaroni
- 2½ cup thick white sauce (see page 46)
- 1½ cup grated cheddar cheese

Method:

1. Boil 8½ cups (2 liters) of water and add the macaroni. Cook until tender and then drain well.
2. After making the white sauce, add half the grated cheese and stir until smooth and creamy.
3. Add the drained macaroni to the sauce and mix well. If the mixture seems too thick, add a bit more milk.
4. Pour the mixture into a lightly buttered baking dish. Sprinkle the rest of the grated cheese evenly over the top.
5. Bake on the middle shelf of the preheated oven for 30 minutes.
6. Serve hot with a salad.

ROAST CHICKEN

Chicken can be roasted many ways. The amount of time it takes to cook, and the number of people it serves, depends on its weight. Here is a roast chicken recipe using the fast-roasting method:

Cook time: 20 minutes for every pound (0.5 kg), plus 20 minutes
**Preheat oven: 425°F
(220°C)**

Ingredients:

- 1 chicken
- Butter

Method:

1. Place the chicken on a rack in a roasting pan, breast up. Rub butter over the breast. Cover loosely with foil. Place near the top of the preheated oven.
2. Remove the foil for the last 15 to 20 minutes.
3. When the chicken is done, allow it to sit for five minutes before carving. Make sure the chicken is cooked thoroughly! NEVER eat undercooked chicken.

BASIC SPONGE CAKE AND ICING OPTIONS
Prep time: 15 minutes
Cook time: 20 minutes
Preheat oven: 375°F (190°C)

Ingredients:
- 2 medium eggs
- ½ cup all-purpose flour
- ¼ cup granulated sugar
- 1 tablespoon hot water

Method:
1. Rub butter around the inside of a 6 to 7 inch (15 to 18 cm) cake pan, then lightly coat with flour and set aside.
2. Crack the eggs and put in a large mixing bowl with the sugar. Whisk together until the mixture is thick and creamy.
3. Add the baking powder to the flour and then sift it to make sure it is very fine and smooth.
4. Slowly add the flour to the egg and sugar mixture, folding it in carefully with a metal spoon. Then, add the water and blend.
5. Spoon the mixture into the greased and floured pan and smooth over the top.
6. Bake in the middle of the preheated oven. Test that the cake is cooked by pressing the top with your finger. If it springs back, the cake is done.
7. Let the cake cool for two to three minutes in the pan before you turn it out onto a wire rack to cool. The cake can be iced when cooled. It can be split into layers and iced between as well as on top. Jam and/or whipped cream can be used instead of icing.

Powdered sugar icing:
Put 2 cups of powdered sugar in a medium bowl. Gradually beat in enough liquid to create a smooth icing that can coat the back of a spoon. The liquid can be water, milk, cream, or fruit juice. Flavorings or food coloring can be added. This type of icing will cover the surface of the cake and run down the sides.

Butter cream frosting
Beat 9 tablespoons of butter or margarine with a wooden spoon or an electric mixer until creamy. Gradually add 1½ to 1¾ cups of powdered sugar. Add 1 to 2 tablespoons of water to make a spreading consistency. Flavorings and food coloring can be added. Spread the frosting onto the cake as thickly as you want using a frosting spatula. It can also be put between layers.

QUIZ RESULTS

QUIZ 1
(Page 13)

Can you decode a recipe?
1) b 2) c 3) a

QUIZ 2
(Page 21)

Can cooking be dangerous?
1) False 2) b 3) c

QUIZ 3
(Page 27)

Can you plan a meal?
1) False 2) a 3) b

20 IMPORTANT COOKING TERMS

1 Bake—cook using dry heat in an oven

2 Baste—moisten food, especially meat, while it is cooking

3 Blanch—immerse food in boiling water for a short period of time and then remove

4 Boil—cook in water at 212°F (100°C)

5 Brown—cook food, usually by frying, sautéing, or roasting, until it is brown in color

6 Dice—chop finely into small cubes

7 Dissolve—make a solution by mixing an ingredient with a liquid

8 Drain—remove something from the liquid it has been stored or cooked in

9 Fry—cook directly over heat in fat or oil

10 Julienne—style of food, especially vegetables, cut into very thin strips

11 Marinate—soak food in a liquid mixture before cooking or serving

12 Pare—remove by cutting or trimming off the outer covering of an ingredient

13 Peel—same as pare

14 Puree —mash, sieve, or use a blender or similar equipment, to make ingredients smooth or liquid

15 Roast—cook in dry heat, usually in an oven

16 Rub in—work the ingredients together with your fingers

17 Simmer—cook just at or just below the boiling point, a gentle boil

18 Steam—cook in the steam of hot or boiling water

19 Stir-fry—cook quickly in a small amount of oil at a high temperature, while at the same time stirring the ingredients to stop them from burning

20 Whisk—blend quickly or whip to a froth

FURTHER INFORMATION

BOOKS

Ballard, Carol. *Food for Feeling Healthy* (*Making Healthy Food Choices*). Chicago: Heinemann Library, 2007.

Barham, Peter. *The Science of Cooking*. New York: Springer, 2001.

King, Hazel. *Food Ingredients* (*Trends in Food Technology*). Chicago: Heinemann Library, 2008.

King, Hazel. *Safe Food* (*Trends in Food Technology*). Chicago: Heinemann Library, 2008.

SOME BASIC COOKBOOKS

Eddy, Jackie. *The Absolute Beginner's Cookbook: Or, How Long Do I Cook a Three-Minute Egg?* New York: Gramercy, 2003.

Exploring History Through Simple Recipes (12-book series). Mankato, Minn.: Capstone, 2008.

Oliver, Jamie. *Cook with Jamie: My Guide to Making You a Better Cook*. New York: Hyperion, 2007.

Stern, Sam. *Cooking up a Storm*. Cambridge, Mass.: Candlewick, 2006.

Stewart, Martha. *Martha Stewart's Cooking School: Lessons and Recipes for the Home Cook*. New York: Clarkson Potter, 2008.

Watt, Fiona. *The Usborne Beginner's Cookbook*. Tulsa, Okla.: Usborne, 2007.

Westmoreland, Susan. *Good Housekeeping Step-by-Step Cookbook*. New York: Hearst, 2008.

WEBSITES

http://mypyramid.gov
This is the official website describing the "MyPyramid" food pyramid.

www.nutrition.gov
This website of the U.S. Department of Agriculture gives diet advice, nutrition facts, information about shopping, cooking, and meal planning, and more.

http://busycooks.about.com/od/cookinglessons/u/Cooking101.htm
This website has recipes and instructions plus lots of advice.

http://allrecipes.com/Recipes/Everyday-Cooking/Quick-and-Easy/Main.aspx
This website offers a wide range of quick and easy recipes.

www.grilling-recipes.com/index.html
This website has a wealth of grilling recipes.

GLOSSARY

accelerant material that increases the speed or intensifies the temperature at which something burns

alkaloid bitter tasting, nitrogen-containing compound

apprentice person who learns a trade while working for someone who is already skilled or qualified

bacteria microscopic one-celled organisms that can cause diseases

carbohydrate compound of carbon, hydrogen, and oxygen, found in sugar and starchy foods

carbon footprint effect an individual has on Earth's environment in terms of the carbon dioxide emissions resulting from his or her lifestyle

contaminate when a material is made impure or unsuitable after contact with something unclean or polluted

cross-contamination when contamination spreads from one thing to another

Crusades military campaigns during the 11th, 12th, and 13th centuries by European Christians against Muslims in the Holy Land

cuisine style or type of cooking, such as Italian cuisine

culinary related to cooking or kitchens

E. coli bacteria *Escherichia coli*, which can cause severe gastric symptoms in people, occasionally resulting in death

epicure someone who is known for his or her knowledge or enjoyment of good food

five food groups food groups that appear on the food pyramid: (1) grains (2) vegetables (3) fruits (4) milk (5) meat and beans. Oils should also be consumed in moderation.

green wood wood on a tree that is still growing and contains sap, making it unlikely to burn

immune system body system that protects a person from infection and disease

industrial espionage one company spying on another to get its secrets

ingredient element that is combined with others to create a mixture

junk food food that is not high in nutrients

kebab pieces of food cooked on a skewer

molecule smallest unit in an element or compound

MyPyramid food pyramid visual representation of the amounts of food that a person should consume from the five major food groups (plus oils). The largest part of the pyramid shows those foods that should be eaten the most, with the smallest part containing those foods that should be eaten in small quantities.

nutritional value food with high nutritional value that sustains or promotes health

obese very overweight

organic grown without the use of synthetic pesticides, fertilizers, or drugs

pesticide residue pesticide material left behind on crops

process treat or prepare a product in a manufacturing or mass-producing environment

protein substance that is a necessary part of the human diet, found in meat, eggs, milk, and some vegetables

raising agent product used in baking to cause a mixture to expand and become light

reality television programs that show real people in real situations

recipe instructions for making a food dish

salmonella bacteria of the genus *Salmonella* that enter the human digestive system through contaminated food, causing severe gastric symptoms and occasionally death

tagine pot heavy clay or cast-iron pot with a circular bottom part and a high, domed lid. It is used especially for cooking North African dishes.

utensil instrument or vessel used in the kitchen for cooking or serving food

wok large, bowl-shaped metal pan used in Chinese and other cooking, particularly for stir-frying

Index